The Art of Chill

How to Stay Cool, Calm and Collected No Matter What

M Salek
Host of *The Better Mindset Show*

***

Disclaimer

This guide is intended for educational purposes only, and not as professional advice. You should always do your own research and decide for yourself before making any decisions, and seek professional advice where relevant.

***

Feedback and suggestions

I really do appreciate you getting this guide. It means a lot to me, seriously. I do the work that I do around mindset, personal growth and peak performance for one reason and one reason only - to help improve people's lives. That's the reason that has kept me doing this work day in and day out for many years now. And hearing about my readers, listeners and students' results and the positive changes they experience through my work never ceases to excite me. I won't be coy about this, I really enjoy getting those emails and messages about how my teachings have improved people's lives!. So, don't feel shy about reaching out to me to share the impact this guide had/is having in your life. You can reach me directly through email at growthphilosophypodcast@gmail.com, and also at my Facebook page. All the best with your personal journey!

Table of Content

Introduction & Why it Matters

I bet you're a bit like me.

Like me, you have had moments in your life when you have lost your cool. Times when you're not really calm or collected. And times when you said things in the heat of the moment which you regretted later.

We have all had experiences like those. I don't know about you, but I personally have had quite a few experiences like that.

Hot headed.

That's what I was known for throughout most of my formative years.

Anger has been a big part of my identity for most of my life. It's not something I am proud of, but neither is it something I feel bad about, because it is what it is and what's done is done. It had its perks, and challenges. If I am being completely honest though, it created more challenges than solutions, which is what led me to focus on learning how to manage my emotions.

And let me tell you that it has not been easy. It has been a long road, and thankfully, I have gotten much better at the whole cool, calm and collected thing. And that journey is what has led to this book, because I wanted to share my own learnings and hard earned insights to help others.

I wish I had known these insights back in the day, as they would have made my life easier, so I plan to do the next best thing and share them with my readers, so that they can benefit from my struggles and lessons.

But let's be honest, my journey isn't that important for you. What is really important is how this book will help you. So let's get into that more.

Why does it matter so much to keep chill and be cool, calm, and collected - especially when things get tough?

There are lots of reasons why.

- It's because that helps you think things through.
- Because it makes it easier to find solutions.
- And also because it makes things less frustrating, overwhelming and stressful.

There are other benefits too. But what it all comes down to is that being able to be cool, calm and collected in the face of stressful situations and settings and scenarios makes your life easier.

And your life being easier is a great thing, as I am sure you will agree.

That's the whole goal of the book - help you be more cool, calm and collected, no matter the situation.

This is not a big book. The fact of the matter is that you can even finish this book in a matter of hours. A lot of effort, focus and attention has gone into making sure that the book is simple, straightforward and easy for you to get through.

Why?

Because, the last thing you need is yet another book that will collect dust and become nothing more than ornament. If this ends up being yet another book in your bookshelf (either physical or digital) that you never get through, then it will be of no value to you.

You don't want that, and I don't want that either.

The whole reason why I put pen to paper and put in all this effort is to help you make your life better. And to that end, I have kept this book simple.

Very simple.

You can easily go through this book in one sitting, in a matter of hours, and then focus on how you can apply to your own life what you learned. I have even added a checklist to make the application easier for you.

All you need to do now is read the book, focus on how you will apply to your own life what you learned, and then get started.

If you apply even just one thing that you take away from this book, even one insight, that will still have a positive impact in your life for many years to come. I have zero doubt that the insights in this book *will* help you.

Now all that remains to be done is for you to read through the book, take note of the insights, and apply what you learn.

Let's begin.

Shift From Reactive to Proactive

The difference between proactive and reactive people is that proactive people design their own destiny, while reactive people simply let life happen to them - Stephen Covey

***

When it comes to being cool, calm and collected, one of the biggest struggles - if not *the* biggest struggle - is being reactive. Being reactive alone can completely derail your ability to be cool, calm and collected, especially during high pressure situations.

Just imagine this - you are at a movie theatre or a mall, and there is a fire. The staff are urging people to stay calm and head for the exit in an orderly fashion.

What do you imagine happens, an orderly move towards the direction of the exit?

Highly unlikely. As tragic as it may seem, it was very likely pandemonium. If you have ever experienced a high pressure situation like that in real life, then you have first-hand experience of this.

For far too many people, when a situation gets hairy or scary or dangerous, common sense seems to fly out the window. They give in to panic and fear and worry, and react in ways that ultimately aren't very good for them.

This is the key difference between being reactive, and proactive. Being reactive is all about losing your head when things go wrong (or seem like they're going to go wrong). Being proactive, on the other hand, is about staying calm and level headed, no matter what happens.

It's about accepting that things aren't always going to go as planned, that things might even go out of control, but even then the smart thing to do is to not give in to your fears when uncertainties like those do crop up.

One of the hardest and maybe even the most unpleasant facts about life is that there are more things in life that you can't control than those that you can. What you can control in life is actually a very small percentage.

Most things in life are, in fact, beyond your control. But that's not the end of the world, because there are some very important things in life that you can control. And one of those few important things in life that you can control is who you are, and what kind of person you want to be.

Unfortunately, most people don't know or realise this. Most people don't give any thought to what kind of person they want to be. While growing up you are often asked about what you want to do in life, but rarely ever (if ever) are you asked about what kind of person you want to be. Our focus becomes pretty much all centred towards external factors, factors like what kind of career you want, where you want to live, and so on and so forth.

However, little to no attention is paid to the vital aspect of your personality, and who you want to be. This aspect is generally considered to be something that is beyond the scope of your control, and you go through life pretty much reacting to what happens around us.

That sort of external focus blinds you to something that is so immensely impactful and valuable that it can not just improve your life, it can even transform your life. And it's the fact that who you are isn't completely beyond your control.

Waking up to this reality can have all sorts of positive impact on your life, namely:

1. It will help you feel more in control, and gain more control over your life
2. It will help you deal with things better, especially the challenging things
3. It helps you make decisions that are better for you
4. It makes your big and small decisions in life simpler, and easier
5. It will help you improve your mental health, physical wellbeing, and even the overall quality of your life.

Here's an example to help you understand this concept better: let's say you deliberately decide that you are going to be the kind of person who prioritises doing good. When you make that decision, most (if not all) of your future decisions become significantly easier, as you will know right away which option is the best one for you, as the option that aligns with that decision about doing good is clearly going to be the one to go for.

Priorities become clearer when you are clear on what kind of person you want to and will be. Other big decisions in life, like the direction to take, your goals, careers, and so on become simpler too. Making this deliberate decision and having this clarity will even make your small day-to-day actions and decisions simpler and easier.

There are lots of benefits to deliberately deciding what kind of person you want to be.

You know that saying, the one about how everyone has a plan until they get punched in the face? That is very true when it comes to your behaviour. Not having a focal point or not explicitly deciding who you want to be is like getting into a car without having any route in mind. Doing that is the most surefire way to get lost, or at the very least, for the journey to be more challenging and even more confusing than it needs to be.

Most people go through life without ever answering that question. Most people never ask themselves what kind of person they want to be. They go through life basically assuming that their personality, behaviours and who they are is a product of circumstances. It is all left to external factors, to things that are out of their control.

This is the thought process that gives rise to the belief that you have no control over who you are. This is why most people go through life being reactive, rather than proactive, especially when it comes to their actions and behaviours. However, that could not be further from the truth. And the truth is that you do have a lot of say over who you are as a person.

One of the most important things in life that you do have control over is what type of person you are. As for getting started, it all comes down to you deliberately and actively deciding who you want to be. When you deliberately decide that you want to be a good person, for example, it will become easier to stick to that decision even when things get hard.

On the other hand, not consciously and deliberately deciding what type of person you will be makes it easier for you to be all over the place any time things get difficult.

What kind of person you want to be is important to know, because this insight has a big impact on how you do things and how you live your life. You can do what most people do and be passive about who you are, or you can take back control over this vitally important part of your life and deliberately and actively decide what kind of person you want to be.

Most people never really think about this. *Most people live their lives without deliberately deciding what type of person they want to and will be.* This is why many people fall off the wagon anytime things get hard.

This is also why people do things that are completely out of character, or even unconscionable. They do it because they have no inner guideline, and no clarity on the type of person they want to be.

Things become much better though when you do have this clarity. In fact, the world would be a much better place than it is right now if more people actively decide what type of people they want to be, or even better, when they actively decide that they want to be good.

The truth is that once you have clarity and conviction about being a good person, living a good life becomes simpler. That answer can make things immensely more clear, and make your choices a whole lot simpler and easier.

When you know clearly who you want to be, you will know what choices align with that parameter and what doesn't. It makes the journey of life a whole lot simpler, easier, and more enjoyable.

It has all sorts of positive impact on your life, making this decision. Things just become simpler and uncomplicated when you know that piece of information. There's a lot less confusion or second guessing involved when you have that clarity about yourself. What's more, that decision can become a powerful compass for your life.

Even though most things in life are completely beyond your control, one of the few things in life that you do have control over is the type of person you are, and will be. It might not seem like the case since you grow up with giving zero thought to the kind of person you are, and generally take it for granted that the type of person you are is something that's a result of what happens in and around us.

But the reality is that you do have a say in the type of person you are, and will be. You do have control over this crucially important aspect of your life, which is a great thing.

And it all starts by deliberately deciding the type of person you want to be.

So here's a question to ask yourself today: What kind of person do you want to be - one who lets situations dictate how they react, or the type of person who thinks things through and grounds themselves and works on staying calm?

I hope you opted for the second option, because that is key to helping you deal with challenging situations well. And that is crucial if you genuinely want to be cool, calm and collected when things get hard.

Don't be reactive because that just is not the smart thing to do.

Be proactive instead.

Stay Focused on What Matters

Worrying is like a rocking chair, it gives you something to do,
but it gets you nowhere - Glenn Turner

***

As far as staying calm (and being proactive rather than reacting to everything) is concerned, one of the behaviours that really helps is focusing on what matters.

For example, if there is a fire in a supermarket you are in, you can react and panic and try to rush to the exit. That, more often than not, will get you injured. Ask any emergency personnel and they will tell you how panic is more dangerous than an actual emergency.

On the other hand, if you focus on what matters - which in that instance will be about being safe - then you will not give in to panic. If you focus on what really matters, then it will be easier for you to pause and think about your next steps.

Doing that and focusing on your next steps (which is what really matters in that scenario) is infinitely better than giving into panic and rushing the exit like far too many people have a tendency of doing. There are emergency protocols for scenarios like those for a reason, and using them generally helps you more than giving in to blind fear.

When life throws you a curveball, it can be easy to get caught up in the chaos and lose sight of what really matters. Whether it's a health emergency, a financial crisis, or a global pandemic, it can be incredibly easy to get bogged down in the stress, worry and anxiety of the situation.

However, it's precisely in those moments of turmoil that it's most important for you to focus on what truly matters. In this chapter, you will explore why it's crucial to keep your focus on the things that are most important in stressful, worrying and challenging times, and how to do so effectively.

Picture this for a second: you're walking through a dark forest, and suddenly, you hear rustling in the bushes. Your heart races as you start to panic - is it a bear? A wolf? A creepy clown? (Okay, maybe not a clown, but you get the idea.)

In moments like these, it's easy to lose sight of what truly matters. Your mind starts to race, and you may find yourself focusing on all the worst-case scenarios. But here's the thing - when things get hairy, scary, or even downright terrifying, it's more important than ever to focus on what really, truly matters.

Let's look into the reasons. The first reason why it is essential to focus on what matters in difficult times is that it helps you to stay grounded, focused and centred. Any time you allow your thoughts and emotions to spiral out of control, it can be difficult to stay present and focused on what's really important.

But if you intentionally direct your attention to the things that truly matter, you can regain a sense of control and balance. By keeping your focus on what truly matters - like your safety and the safety of those around you - you're less likely to get overwhelmed by fear and panic.

It's not just about staying calm in the face of danger though. Focusing on what matters can also help you make better decisions in all areas of your life. When you're able to cut through the noise and distractions and zero in on what's truly important, you can make more proactive choices that align with your values and goals.

Additionally, focusing on what matters helps you to maintain perspective. When you're caught up in a crisis, it's easy to lose sight of the bigger picture and get bogged down in the details. However, by keeping your attention on the things that are most important, you can take a step back and assess the situation from a more comprehensive and logical perspective.

This shift in focus, in turn, can help you to make more informed decisions, and can also help you see opportunities that you might otherwise have missed.

Another reason why it's vital to focus on what matters in high pressure situations is that it helps you to maintain your sense of purpose. When you are facing a crisis, it's easy to feel overwhelmed and hopeless, and to question whether anything you do really matters. However, by staying connected to the things that truly matter to you, you can stay focused on your goals, and continue to move forward even in the face of adversity.

So how can you stay focused on what matters when things get hairy, scary, or worrying? One effective strategy is to create a daily practice of reflection and intention setting. By taking just a few minutes each day to reflect on your values and priorities, and set clear intentions for the day ahead, you can stay connected to the things that matter the most to you, even when you're feeling overwhelmed or distracted.

Another technique that is helpful is to practise gratitude. When you take the time to appreciate the good things in your life, even in the middle of challenging situations, it helps remind you of what truly matters, and how there is good in your life even when things get hard. Gratitude can also help to shift your perspective from one of scarcity to one of abundance, which can be incredibly empowering in challenging times.

A third technique that will help is to practise mindfulness. By staying present and focused on the here and now, you can avoid getting caught up in worries about the future or regrets about the past. This can help you stay centred and focused on what truly matters in the moment. You will learn more about this in the chapter on present focus.

Here is the bottom line - at the end of the day, it's easy to get caught up in the chaos of life. But by staying focused on what truly matters, you can weather any storm that comes your way. That focus will help you from getting bogged down by the chaos and noise, and stay focused on what matters. So, the next time you find yourself in a hairy, scary, or even a downright terrifying situation, remember to take a deep breath, stay focused, and keep your eyes on the prize.

See the Glass Half Full

The optimist sees opportunity in every difficulty - Winston Churchill

***

Glass half full or half empty - you have no doubt heard that phrase in one shape or another. It comes up often in connection with being optimistic or pessimistic. The idea behind it is that people who are more optimistic find it easier to see the glass half full. But it works the opposite way for people who are more pessimistic, as they tend to focus on the negative and see the glass as half empty rather than half full.

Same glass, but two *very* different perspectives.

This is a classic example of how you can choose to see things in either a positive or negative light. But here's the thing: choosing to see the glass as half full can actually make a big difference in how you navigate through life's ups and downs.

Let's face it, life can be tough. There are always going to be challenges, struggles and obstacles that come your way. And when things get hairy, scary, or even downright terrifying, it can be easy to get sucked into a negative mindset. But what if I told you that choosing to be optimistic could actually help you stay cool, calm, and collected no matter what?

Here is how that works: when you focus on the positive, you are more likely to see opportunities instead of struggles. Then you become more resilient and better able to bounce back from setbacks. And when you believe that things will work out for the best, you are more likely to take risks and try new things.

It works the other way too, because when you focus on the negative, you are more likely to see struggles rather than opportunities. Then it becomes easier to give in to feelings like hopelessness and despair. Because if you don't believe that things will work out, then you will live in a state of fear and hopelessness.

As you can tell, focusing on the positive is the better approach. Because that positive focus helps you get more in life. This is why focusing on the positive is vital if you want to be cool, calm and collected when things get hard.

One of the main objections when it comes to optimism and positive focus is that it is not realistic. But that's a misconception. Here's the thing, optimism doesn't mean ignoring reality or being unrealistic.

Not at all.

Optimism is not really about wearing rose-tinted glasses and ignoring the negative. Instead, it is about focusing on the positive while acknowledging the negative. This approach makes it possible for people to stay grounded in reality while also looking for opportunities and solutions to problems. In short, being optimistic helps people to stay cool, calm, and collected, no matter what life throws at them.

Being optimistic helps you deal with challenging situations well, that is one of its biggest benefits, and is reason enough to practise optimism. But there are others too. One of the biggest benefits of optimism, in fact, is that it can help improve your health.

Studies have shown that optimists tend to have lower levels of stress, lower blood pressure, and a stronger immune system. What's more, optimism has been linked to longer life expectancy, with one study showing that optimists live an average of seven and a half years longer than pessimists.

Optimism can also have a positive impact on relationships. Here is a phenomenon you have very likely noticed yourself - people tend to be drawn to optimistic people, as they tend to give off positivity, uplifting and good energy. Additionally, optimists tend to have better communication skills and are more likely to resolve conflicts in a positive way.

And that then makes it possible for them to have stronger and more fulfilling relationships, both at work and at home. As Mary Lou Retton put it: Optimism is a happiness magnet. If you stay positive, good things and good people will be drawn to you.

Another benefit of optimism is a higher level of resilience. Optimists tend to view setbacks, obstacles and challenges as temporary and surmountable, rather than permanent and insurmountable. They know that no obstacle is impossible to overcome.

This mindset makes it possible for optimistic people to bounce back from adversity more quickly and easily. But in contrast, pessimists tend to view setbacks as permanent and insurmountable, leading to feelings of despair, helplessness and hopelessness.

Clearly, optimism is the better option.
So how can you become more optimistic and develop a "glass-half-full" mindset? Here are three things that can really help:
1. Be mindful of your thoughts. This will make it easier for you to nip the negative thoughts before they get a chance to take over your mind.
2. Actively work on reframing negative thoughts into positive ones. For example, instead of dwelling on a setback, focus on the lessons you learned and the opportunities for growth.
3. Work on surrounding yourself with positive people.Because the people around you have a big impact on your state of mind.
4. Take care of your health. Because it is easier to feel optimistic when you're feeling youll. More on this in the "Nurture Your Trifecta" chapter.
5. Do things that bring you joy and fulfilment.

Here is the bottom line - being optimistic is about choosing to focus on the good while acknowledging the bad. It is about accepting the problems and then looking for solutions. It is also about seeing the glass as half full and looking for ways to fill it up even more. And when you do this, you create a positive feedback loop that can help you stay motivated, energised, and engaged.

Get into the habit of seeing the glass half full. And the next time you're faced with a challenge, obstacle or setback, try to see the glass as half full. Look for the opportunities, lessons and possibilities that exist, even in the middle of difficulty. And remember, optimism is a choice that you can all make. So why not choose to focus on the positive and see where it takes you?

Beware the Expectation Trap

Expectations are like fine pottery. The harder you hold them, the more likely they are to crack - Brandon Sanderson

***

One of the biggest challenges with being cool, calm and collected has to do with the expectations that you have.

The thing is, expectations are hard to avoid completely. They are part of your day to day life. We expect things from ourselves, from others, and even from the universe. Sometimes these expectations are helpful and lead to positive outcomes, but other times they can lead you down a path of disappointment, dismay and even distress.

This is where the expectation trap comes in. This happens when you hold on too tightly to your expectations, even when they're not realistic, useful or helpful, and end up feeling let down and defeated.

If you are tired of constantly feeling disappointed and let down by the world around you, then you have experienced the expectation trap first hand. Let's face it, we've all fallen into the expectation trap at some point in our lives. We set our sights on a goal or an ambition or a dream, only to have it fall short of our expectations.

It's easy to feel defeated and frustrated when things don't go your way.

It's easy, but it is not good. It is not good because letting your expectations dictate how you feel and act is a recipe for disaster. Falling into the expectation trap is a surefire way to get held back in life, and it is one of the worst things you can do if you want to be cool, calm and collected in the face of adversity.

If you let your expectations decide how you feel, it will be easy to feel dejected, down and even depressed any time things don't quite work out as expected. And as you know by now, life is never guaranteed and things don't always work out as expected. This is why letting your expectations have the last say is not just a recipe for struggle and unhappiness, it is also absolutely unrealistic.

Long story short, falling into the expectation trap and letting your expectations decide how you feel, think and act is not a smart thing to do. And it most certainly isn't going to help if you want to deal with challenging situations calmly.

So how can you avoid the expectation trap? First, you need to recognize when you are setting unrealistic expectations for yourself or others. Are you expecting too much too soon? Are you basing your expectations on things you can't control? Are you creating unrealistic stories of what should happen, and so on?

Once you identify these expectations, you can begin to adjust them and focus on what's factually achievable.

Another effective strategy for avoiding the expectation trap is being able to adapt and adjust your expectations as circumstances change. The thing is, life is never predictable. There are times when things don't work out as planned. That's the bad news.

The good news is that if you're able to stay flexible and pivot and shift your expectations, it will be easier for you to avoid feeling like your life is spiralling out of control. That also means that managing your expectations will go a long way in helping you stay cool, calm and collected no matter the situation.

It's also useful to reframe how you think about expectations. So instead of focusing on what you want to happen, you can shift your attention to what you can control in the present moment. This will help you stay grounded and centred, even in the face of uncertainty.

It's important to remember that avoiding falling into the expectation trap is worth the effort. For one, it can lead to increased stress and anxiety. When you're constantly fixated on what you want to happen, you're not able to fully appreciate and engage with the present moment. This can also negatively impact your relationships with others, as you may become resentful or disappointed when they don't meet your expectations.

What's good though is that when you're able to let go of unrealistic expectations and focus on what's achievable, you can cultivate a sense of contentment, appreciation and peace of mind. That also helps you become more resilient and adaptable, and capable of handling whatever life throws your way with strength and ease.

In summary, avoiding the expectation trap is all about being able to accept, adapt and adjust your expectations as circumstances change, and focusing on what you can control in the present moment. By doing that, you can nurture a sense of peace, resilience and gratitude, and stay cool, calm, and collected no matter what life throws your way.

The more expectations you have, the easier it will become for you to get triggered, it really is as simple as that. That said, it's not easy to not have any expectations. However, working on managing and limiting your expectations will help you to be cool, calm, and collected even in the face of the most challenging of situations. And that makes this something worth working on.

Remember, life is full of surprises and unexpected ups and downs, and twists and turns. There are no guarantees that things will always meet your expectations. But by learning to manage your expectations, you can stay calm and centred no matter what.

So, the next time you find yourself setting unrealistic expectations, try shifting your focus to acceptance, appreciation and growth. You may be surprised at how much more relaxed, calm and positive you feel!

Embrace the Unexpected

Life is 10% what happens to you and 90% how you react to it - Charles R. Swindoll

***

Here is one of the biggest truths about life - unexpected things happen. And they happen a lot. That's one of the main reasons why people struggle to stay cool, calm and collected. Life is a beautiful yet unpredictable journey, full of unexpected twists and turns. No matter how much you plan or prepare, there will always be surprises waiting for you around the corner.

These curveballs can knock you off your feet, leaving you feeling confused, overwhelmed and stressed. It's no wonder that staying cool, calm, and collected is a challenge for many.

Just think back to the last time you were thrown a curveball. Maybe your plans got unexpectedly cancelled, or something you expected to happen did not happen, or perhaps you received some shocking news.

When the unexpected happens, it can be easy to feel overwhelmed, stressed, and anxious. But what if I told you that embracing the unexpected can help you stay cool, calm, and collected no matter what comes your way?

Even if that sounds hard to believe, embracing the unexpected really does have an impact on your capacity to deal with things well. Because the alternative, resisting the unexpected, does not really change anything but does make things harder.

Like it or not, life is unpredictable. No matter how much you prepare and plan, there will always be unexpected things that you just cannot control. But instead of fighting against them, you can learn to embrace them. By accepting the unexpected, you can shift your mindset and adapt to new situations more easily.

Embracing the unexpected can also help you become more resilient. Here is how that works - when you are faced with unexpected challenges, you have the opportunity to learn and grow from them. By reframing those challenges as opportunities for growth, you can approach them with a positive, productive and proactive mindset. Doing this, in turn, can help you build resilience, and bounce back from difficult situations more easily.

What's more, embracing the unexpected can open you up to new experiences and possibilities. When you let go of your expectations of how things should be and embrace the unknown, you can discover new passions, make new connections, and learn new skills. These experiences can enrich your life and help you grow as a person.

For all these reasons and more, embracing the unexpected is a very useful habit to adopt. But how can you embrace the unexpected? It all begins with shifting your mindset. Instead of fearing the unknown, you can choose to approach it with curiosity, impartiality and openness.

You can also practise mindfulness and live in the present moment. When you are fully present, you can more easily adapt to new situations and make decisions from a place of calm and clarity. Read more about this in the chapter on becoming present focused.

Here is what it all comes down to - life can throw you curveballs when you least expect it, and sometimes it can be downright scary. But trying to fight or resist the unexpected does not really help. What does help is embracing the unexpected.

Embracing the unexpected is about being open to change. And it is also about seeing the unexpected situations as opportunities for growth and learning. By shifting your mindset, practising mindfulness, and embracing new experiences, you can become more adaptable, resilient, and open-minded.

Accepting the unexpected is one of the best things you can do to stay cool, calm and collected. It's normal to want to have certainty, because uncertainty feels uncomfortable. That said, the more you train yourself to become comfortable with uncertainties and embrace the unexpected, the easier it will be for you to stay cool, calm, and collected no matter what happens.

Embracing the unexpected can be scary at first, but it can also add excitement and adventure to your life. By learning to roll with the punches and approach the unexpected with an open mind, you can stay calm and adapt to any situation.

It's harder to do in the beginning, but does get easier the more you practise it. And that makes actively practising going with the flow, letting things be and becoming comfortable with uncertainties a worthwhile trait to develop. So the next time life throws you a curveball, embrace it with open arms and see where it takes you.

Get into the habit of embracing the unexpected.

Stay Ahead of the Game

By failing to prepare, you are preparing to fail - Benjamin Franklin

***

Being cool, calm and collected is a great place to be in. But it isn't an easy one. Let's face it, if it was easy, everyone would be cool, calm and collected all the time, but that's hardly ever the case. As you have been learning so far, there are quite a few things that can get in the way of your ability to be cool, calm and collected under pressure. You have been learning about ways to tackle these challenges as well.

Carrying on that thread, another major obstacle to your ability to stay cool, calm and collected is the lack of information on what your alternatives or the next steps will be anytime things don't go according to plan. That lack of clarity can confuse you, which then creates more uncertainty, and that then feeds your fear mechanism and makes it harder for you to stay composed.

Imagine being in the middle of a maze without a map or any signs to guide you - that's how it feels when unexpected things happen and you're left in the dark about what to do next. The lack of information can quickly turn into confusion, uncertainty, and fear, making it challenging to keep a level head.

But here's the good news: by taking the time to understand your alternatives and prepare for the unexpected, you can navigate any obstacle with confidence, competence and composure.

This is why when it comes to dealing with life's ups and downs, preparation is crucially important. Because being prepared helps you stay ahead of the game, and also helps you deal with uncertainties calmly, composedly and confidently, no matter what life throws at you.

Picture this: you're at the beach, soaking up the sun, feeling all relaxed, chill and carefree. You take a stroll along the shore, enjoying the sights and sounds of the ocean. Suddenly, a huge wave comes crashing down on you, drenching you from head to toe.

What do you do? Panic and run for cover? Or stand your ground, shake off the water, and keep strolling along the beach?

Life can be like that giant wave, full of unexpected twists and turns that can leave you feeling drenched and overwhelmed. But with a little preparation, you can stay ahead of the game and ride the waves of life with ease.

Whatever the situation, be it a health problem or a personal crisis or problems at work, being prepared can go a long way in helping you feel more in control, and better able to deal with the uncertainties.

One of the biggest benefits of being prepared is that it can cut down on the level of worry, anxiety and stress you feel. It's like this - when you know what to expect and have a plan in place, you are less likely to feel overwhelmed, clueless or caught off guard. This can then help you stay calm and focused, even in high-pressure situations.

Another benefit of being prepared is that it can help you make better decisions. When you're not rushed, stressed or panicked, you have more time to weigh your options and consider different approaches. This, in turn, can lead to more thoughtful and effective decision-making, which can then help you achieve better outcomes.

Being prepared also makes it possible for you to be more proactive rather than reactive (we covered this in detail in the initial chapter). When you opt for being proactive, you can take a more active approach and anticipate potential challenges instead of simply reacting to whatever comes your way. This can then help you identify and address problems before they become too big to handle, and can also give you a greater sense of control over your own life.

What being prepared does not mean though is obsessing over every little detail or having a rigid plan for every possible scenario. Life is unpredictable, at the end of the day, and unexpected things can and will happen. It's not really possible for you to be prepared for every little thing. And that's not the point. The point is to have a general sense of direction and the tools to handle whatever comes your way.

Even if you can't prepare for each and every thing, having a general plan in place and being mentally and emotionally prepared can help you adapt and respond more effectively to whatever comes your way. Much more effectively than if you don't plan, prepare and work on staying ahead of the game.

Think of it like a hiking trip. You don't know exactly what you'll come across on the trail, but you bring along the essentials - a map, a compass, a first aid kit - to help you navigate any challenges that might crop up.

The same goes for life. By being prepared, you give yourself the confidence to face any situation with calm and clarity. Whether it's a last-minute project at work, a surprise visit from your in-laws, or a sudden change in your health, you'll be able to handle it all with ease.

Preparation matters, it really is as simple as that. The more prepared you are, the easier it gets to deal with life's curveballs. You might not be able to plan and prepare for every single thing in life, but there are lots you can prepare for. The point isn't to be prepared for absolutely everything, but rather to prepare to the best of your abilities. Because even a small amount of preparation is much better than not being prepared at all.

To sum it all up, being prepared is essential for staying ahead of the game and dealing with life's challenges calmly. By reducing anxiety and stress, improving decision-making, and allowing for a more proactive approach, being prepared can help you feel more in control and better equipped to deal with whatever life throws your way. So take some time to prepare yourself for potential challenges ahead.

You'll be glad that you did.

Make Conscious Decisions

When you react, you let others control you. When you respond,
you are in control - Bohdi Sanders

***

Every single day you make hundreds of decisions. This isn't something that you can avoid. From the decision about what to eat to what work to do first and what to wear and many others, your days are full of decisions.

The thing is, most of the decisions you make happen on a subconscious level. They happen automatically. Like your decision to breathe. You can actually decide to not breathe by simply choosing to hold your breath. That's not something you'll want to do, but it proves the point that even something as fundamental as your breathing needs to pass through a decision mechanism.

Thankfully, that sort of fundamental function doesn't need you to actively decide things - they happen automatically. You don't have to consciously decide to breathe, for instance, that decision takes place at your subconscious level, which means that you don't need to think about it.

When it comes to fundamental biological functions like breathing, automated decisions like that are extremely useful. However, that's not useful for every different scenario in your life. And this is where thinking things through and making conscious, active decisions come in.

Making conscious decisions is one of the most crucial skills you can develop in life. You have no doubt met people or heard stories of people who have made impulsive choices that led to disastrous consequences, so you have a fairly good idea about what happens if you give into your knee-jerk reactions.

While some decisions may seem insignificant at the time, they can ultimately impact your entire life. When life gets hard, and the pressure is on, it's tempting to make quick decisions to deal with the discomfort. However, taking a moment to step back and think things through can make all the difference.

When faced with high-pressure situations and difficult decisions, it can be really tempting to take the easy way out and make choices based on your emotions. The thing is, emotions can be deceiving, and they don't always reflect the best course of action. By taking a step back and considering all the options, you can make more informed, objective and rational decisions.

This is especially true when you're under pressure or dealing with challenging circumstances. In situations like that, your mind can easily become clouded, and you might feel overwhelmed, dazed or confused. In situations like that the easy option is to just go with your impulsive, knee-jerk reactions. But doing the opposite and taking a moment to reflect on your options and weighing up the pros and cons is actually the better option since that can help you make the best decision possible.

Thinking things through also makes it possible for you to take a long-term perspective. When you rush to make decisions, you will end up focusing on short-term benefits, and fail to consider the long-term consequences. But by taking the time to think things through, you can consider how your decisions will impact you in the future. You can then weigh up the potential risks and rewards, and make decisions that align with your values, priorities and goals.

Have you ever made a snap decision that turned out to be a complete disaster? Maybe you bought a car without researching the make and model first, or agreed to go on a blind date without even asking what the person looks like. We've all been there, but making impulsive decisions can often leave you in sticky situations. That's why it's important to take a step back, think things through, and make conscious decisions, especially when things get hard.

The more conscious your decisions are, the easier it is for you to keep your head. But it works the other way too, because the more you give in to automated decisions and do things like blindly follow the crowd and not think things through, especially during high pressure situations, the easier it gets to lose your head. That makes thinking things through and making active, well thought out and conscious decisions an essential part of being able to stay cool, calm and collected no matter what.

While it may be tempting to make snap decisions or go with your gut feeling, taking the time to think things through can save you from a ton of headaches in the long run. By seeing the big picture, weighing the pros and cons, and avoiding emotional decisions, you can make conscious, active decisions - decisions that align with your values, priorities and goals.

Remember this, when things get tough, hairy or even scary, making conscious decisions will help you far more than running around like a headless chicken. So make it a point to think before you act, especially when things get hard. And try this the next time you're faced with a tough decision: take a deep breath, grab a pen and paper, and start thinking things through.

Your future self will thank you for it.

Nurture Your Trifecta

Taking care of yourself is the most powerful way to begin to take care of others - Bryant McGill

***

How you feel has a lot to do with your ability to stay cool, calm and collected. Especially when you are faced with challenging situations, not feeling well will make it infinitely harder for you to stay chill, and be cool, calm and collected.

Let's face it, life can be challenging at times, and it is easy to get caught up in the daily grind and forget to take care of yourself. However, it is important to remember that just like pretty much everything in life, you need looking after too. You need to nurture your trifecta, i.e. your mind, body, and soul to stay chill, calm and collected, no matter what life throws your way. In this chapter, you will learn about some important reasons why self-nurturing is so essential, and how you can practise it in your daily life.

The first thing to take note of is the fact that stressful situations can hit you when you least expect it. Maybe you're having a bad day at work, maybe your car was scratched up badly while getting out of your garage, or maybe your cat just ruined your favourite sweater. Whatever the case may be, it's important to remember that taking care of your mind, body, and soul is crucial for staying chill and calm in high-pressure situations.

Think of it this way - when you're on an aeroplane, the flight attendant always tells you to put on your own oxygen mask before helping others. The same goes for dealing with challenging situations. No matter how much you want, you can't help others if you are not looking after yourself first. If you are not in good shape, you can't be there for others effectively, it really is as simple as that.

This is a proven fact, by the way. Research has shown that self-care is essential for overall health and wellbeing. Here are a few key findings to help you understand just how important it is for you to nurture your trifecta:

Better physical health: Self-care practices like regular exercise, healthy eating, and getting enough sleep have been linked to improved physical health, including lower risk of chronic diseases such as heart disease and diabetes.

Less stress and anxiety: Self-care practices such as mindfulness, meditation, and deep breathing have been shown to reduce stress and anxiety levels. In fact, a study published in the Journal of Alternative and Complementary Medicine found that mindfulness-based stress reduction led to significant reductions in symptoms of anxiety, stress and depression.

Increased productivity: Taking time for self-care can actively improve your productivity in the long run. A study published in the Journal of Occupational and Environmental Medicine found that employees who participated in a workplace wellness program that included self-care activities reported increased job satisfaction and productivity.

Better relationships: Self-care practices such as mindfulness, journaling, and spending time with loved ones have been shown to improve relationships and communication skills. When you nurture your trifecta and look after yourself, it becomes easier for you to show up for others in your life.

There are more benefits (lots more), but long story short, research has consistently shown that practising self-care is an important part of maintaining your overall health and wellbeing. This is why nurturing your trifecta is crucial if you want to be chill under pressure, because by taking care of your mind, body, and soul, you will be better able to handle whatever life throws your way.

On that note, you can't just focus on one part of your wellbeing and ignore others. This, unfortunately, is something far too many people do. The thing is, your mind, body, and soul are interconnected, and neglecting one can have a ripple effect on all the others.

For example, if you take care of your mental and emotional wellbeing but neglect your physical health, you may become lethargic and unable to focus, which will then negatively affect your mental and emotional wellbeing. Similarly, if you ignore your emotional needs, you may become stressed and anxious, which can then lead to health problems like headaches, digestive issues and so on.

Taking care of yourself, it goes without saying, is essential. However, that does not mean selfishly putting your needs above others. Not at all. This, by the way, is one of the biggest misconceptions about self care being selfish.

The truth is very different. Because taking care of yourself is simply about understanding that your wellbeing is essential for you to be your best self, especially if you want to help others effectively.

When you prioritise self-care, you are better equipped to handle life's challenges, and you become more resilient. And all that also makes you better equipped to be there for others as well.

Taking care of yourself and nurturing your trifecta is not just good for you, it is also good for others, especially the people who really matter.

So how can you get started? There are lots of ways to nurture your mind, body, and soul. Here are some ideas for you to help give you a head start:

- Taking care of your physical health can involve eating nutritious food, getting regular exercise, and getting enough sleep.

- Mental self-care can involve taking time for hobbies or creative outlets, learning new things, and practising mindfulness or meditation.
- Spiritual self-care can involve practising gratitude, connecting with nature, and helping others.

Now you know why it is important for you to take care of yourself, as well as how you can do that. What is also essential for you to remember though is that self-nurturing and care is not a one-time fix, but a lifelong journey. You need to make a conscious effort to prioritise your wellbeing, and it may take trial and error to find the self-care practices that work best for you. That said, with time and effort, you can build a self-care routine that helps you stay cool, calm, and collected, no matter what life throws your way.

Here's the most important thing to remember about all this - if you're not in good shape (both inside and out), then being cool, calm and collected will be a struggle for you. The weaker you are when it comes to the state of your overall mind, body and soul, the easier it will be to get swept over by challenges.

The good news is that it works the other way too, because the stronger the state of your mind, body and soul is, the easier it will be for you to deal with whatever life throws your way.

Nurturing your trifecta, i.e. your mind, body, and soul, is not a luxury but a necessity if you want to be able to handle life's challenges easily and effectively. By prioritising self-care, you can become more resilient, and better equipped to handle whatever life throws your way. So, take a moment to reflect on your self-care routine and make a conscious effort to nurture yourself each day.

Get into the habit of nurturing your mind, body and soul regularly. Because they are crucial factors in helping you stay chill, no matter what.

Become Present Focused

The secret of health for both mind and body is not to mourn for the past, not to worry about the future, or not to anticipate troubles, but to live in the present moment wisely and earnestly - Buddha

***

Being cool, calm and collected is good for all sorts of reasons. It feels great to be chill, especially when things get hard. However, one of the things that gets in the way of that in a big way is not focusing on the present. What this also means is that shifting your focus can make a big difference in your ability to stay still, and that's what this chapter is all about.

Here's a question for you - do you ever feel like life is pulling you in a million different directions, leaving you feeling stressed, confused and overwhelmed? It's easy to get caught up in worrying about the future or dwelling on the past, but have you ever stopped to consider the power of focusing on the present moment?

When you're facing a challenging situation, it's natural to feel anxious or stressed. But by bringing your attention back to the present moment, you can start to feel more calm and centred. Instead of getting lost in worries about what might happen next or what you should have done differently in the past, you can focus on what's happening right now.

Think about it: when you're fully present in the current moment, you're able to respond to what's happening around you in a much more effective way. You're not weighed down by the weight of past mistakes or worries about the future. Instead, you're able to tap into your intuition, skills and insights and respond to the situation with calm, clarity and confidence.

Focusing on the present also helps you to cultivate a sense of gratitude for the things that are going well in your life right now. The thing is, it is easy to take the good things in your life for granted, especially when you're always focused on what's next. But by actively taking time to appreciate the present moment, you can start to develop a deeper sense of gratitude, happiness and peace.

There is an important point worth clarifying here, which is that focusing on the present moment doesn't mean that you should ignore the past or the future entirely. That's not the point at all. It is important to reflect on the past and make plans for the future, but it is equally (if not more) important to not get lost in those thoughts and let them consume you.

The reality is that both the past and the future have their place in your life. But dwelling too much on either can take you away from the present moment. The past is where you can learn from your experiences, but constantly revisiting it can keep you stuck in negative emotions like regret, shame, or resentment.

Similarly, the future is where you can set goals and plan for the things that you want to achieve. But constantly worrying about it can (and will) bring up feelings of anxiety, fear, and uncertainty.

The key is finding a balance between all three timeframes. Reflecting on the past can give you insights into what you want to improve or what you want to avoid in the future. Planning for the future can help you create a vision for your life and give you direction. But ultimately, the present is where you live your life. That is where you can take action, make changes, and experience all the joys and challenges that come your way.

When you're able to focus on the present moment, you're more likely to be fully engaged in what you're doing, whether it's having a conversation with a friend, focusing on work, or even just enjoying some time on your own. Being present also makes it possible for you to fully experience your emotions without judgement, stress or resistance. That way, instead of trying to avoid or numb your feelings, you can acknowledge them, process them, and let them go.

When it comes to dealing with challenging situations, focusing on the present can help you stay chill and centred. When you're feeling overwhelmed or stressed, it's easy to get caught up in your thoughts and lose sight of what's happening in front of you. But by bringing your attention back to the present moment, you can ground yourself and find a sense of clarity. From there, you can then make decisions or take actions that are aligned with your values, priorities and goals, rather than reacting impulsively based on your emotions.

When faced with challenging situations, it's natural to feel overwhelmed and stressed out. You might find yourself ruminating about the past or worrying about the future, but neither of these actions will help you in the present moment. That's why it's essential to focus on the present if you want to be chill in the face of adversity.

Focusing on the present allows you to let go of regrets about the past and anxiety about the future. It helps you stay grounded and centred, which is essential for maintaining your composure when things get tough.

When you focus on the present, you become more mindful. You pay attention to your thoughts, feelings, and sensations without judgement. This awareness, in turn, allows you to respond to challenges in a calm and rational way instead of reacting impulsively. By focusing on the present, you can take a step back, observe the situation, and choose how you want to respond.

Focusing on the present also helps you stay in control of your emotions. When you're stressed out, your mind can race, and your emotions can get the best of you. But when you focus on the present, you can slow down and take a deep breath. You can identify the source of your stress and decide how to manage it. You can choose to practise self-care, such as meditation, exercise, or spending time with loved ones. You can also choose to take action, such as solving a problem or seeking help.

As you can tell, being present focused comes with all sorts of benefits. And as far as being cool, calm and collected is concerned, that is an extremely useful thing to do.

The key thing to remember here is that the only time that truly exists is the present moment. That is an undeniable fact of life. The past is unchangeable, and the future is uncertain and beyond our control. The only thing you have complete control over is this moment - the here and now.

Focusing on the present helps you stay grounded and deal with challenges, obstacles and uncertainties in a good way. This is why it's a smart idea to adopt the habit of being present focused, because that'll go a long way in helping you stay strong no matter what.

So the next time you're feeling overwhelmed or stressed, try taking a few deep breaths and bringing your attention back to the present moment. Pay attention to your surroundings, notice your thoughts and feelings without judgement, and be grateful for the good things in your life. With a little practice, you might be surprised at just how effective this simple practice can be for helping you feel more chill in the face of challenging situations.

Practice being present focused, especially when things don't go as

planned.

The Help-Seeking Advantage

It's not weak to ask for help. It's a testament to your strength - R.J. Silver

***

Here's one of the most effective things you can do to be more cool, calm and collected. And it is to get help. Especially when things get tough. Easier said than done though, as you know yourself. How that works, and why tapping into the help-seeking advantage is immensely useful when it comes to dealing with difficult situations effectively, is what you will learn about in this chapter. Keep reading.

Do you ever feel like you're drowning in your problems and can't seem to catch a break? Well, guess what? You don't have to go through it alone! Asking for help can be a game changer for you, and can even turn your life around and help you tackle the most challenging situations with a clear and calm mind.

Picture this: you're in a lifeboat in the middle of a raging storm, the waves are crashing against the boat, and you're desperately trying to keep it afloat. You're exhausted, overwhelmed, and feel like giving up. But suddenly, a rescue team arrives and throws you a lifeline. With their help, you're able to get back on track and navigate your way through the storm.

In the same way, asking for help can be your lifeline during the tough times in life. Whether it's a trusted friend, a therapist, or a support group, reaching out and getting the help you need can transform your life. It can help you gain a fresh perspective, process your emotions, and give you the tools you need to cope with whatever life throws your way.

Asking for help is good for all sorts of reasons. But it isn't always easy to do.

One of the biggest reasons behind that is the belief that asking for help makes you weak. Far too many people believe (wrongly) that asking for help makes them weak. They think that asking for help means they are not capable of handling things on their own, and that others will judge them for not being self-sufficient.

This belief can then make them reluctant to ask for help, even when they really need it.This reluctance to ask for help can create a lot of stress, worry and anxiety. It can be overwhelming to try to carry the weight of the world on your shoulders, and it can feel like you're all alone in your struggles.

The truth though is that asking for help has nothing to do with being weak. Because the reality is that it takes courage and strength to admit that you need help.

Asking for help when you're facing a challenging situation can transform your life and help you navigate even the toughest of circumstances with calm and grace. Whether it's getting guidance from a professional, confiding in a friend, or turning to a support group, asking for help is a powerful tool that can help you become more resilient, strong, and even lead to transformational growth.

One of the biggest benefits of asking for help is gaining a new perspective. When you are dealing with a problem, it can be difficult to see a way out. Problems, especially the big ones, have a way to really cloud your mind. But asking for help from someone with an outside perspective can help you see the situation in a new light. What's more, it can even help you find solutions that you may not have considered before.

That's not all. Asking for help can give you a sense of relief and validation. The thing is, when you are in the thick of a challenging situation, it can be easy for you to feel alone and isolated. But by reaching out for help, you are reminded that you are not alone in your struggles. This realisation can then give you a great sense of relief and comfort. This realisation alone can help you in a big way to deal with even the most scary of situations.

Additionally, asking for help can give you the tools and strategies you need to better manage your challenges - both internal and external. Whether it's learning new coping skills or receiving therapy to work through trauma or figuring out how to tackle a tricky work project, asking for help can help you find the resources you need to build resilience and overcome adversity.

Here is the really important thing to remember, and it is that asking for help is not a sign of weakness, but rather a sign of strength. When you are struggling, asking for help is one of the bravest and most important things you can do for yourself. It takes courage to admit that you can't do it alone and that you need help. But in doing so, you open yourself up to new solutions, possibilities and even opportunities for growth.

Asking for and getting help does not make you weak. The notion that going it alone and doing everything on your own is the true sign of strength is pure and utter nonsense. It's an outdated and archaic notion, but more importantly, it's an unhelpful concept that only gets in the way of your life and makes things unnecessarily complicated for you. If anything, asking for and getting help is a good thing and is a sign of strength.

What's more, it makes life easier for you. And most importantly, it makes it easier for you to tackle whatever life throws at you in a cool, calm and collected way. Asking for help isn't a sign of weakness, it's a sign of strength. And it helps you deal with challenges better. So get into the habit of asking for help anytime you need it. Because not doing so is a recipe for making your life unnecessarily more complicated, painful, and hard.

Stop letting outdated notions get in your way. Whenever you need it, ask for help.

Go From Chaos to Clarity

You can't calm the storm, so stop trying. What you can do is calm yourself. The storm will pass - Timber Hawkeye

***

Have you ever found yourself in a situation where everything seems chaotic, stressful and overwhelming? Maybe it was a work project that suddenly got out of hand, or a personal problem that seemed to have no solution. In times like these, it can be easy to feel lost, confused and unsure of what to do next.

But what really helps in situations like those is your ability to get clear on what you need to do. When it comes to your ability to be cool, calm and collected, chaos (especially when it is accompanied by uncertainty and lack of clarity) is one of your biggest obstacles. And the more you lack clarity, the harder it becomes to be cool, calm and collected.

On the other hand, when you have clarity, you can face any situation with level-headedness, confidence and purpose. This doesn't mean that you need to have all the answers right away. No, especially since it is pretty much impossible to have all the answers. No one has all the answers, ever, and that's one truth about life you need to accept.

Going back to the point about chaos, having all the answers is not the point, and that's not what you should aim for since that will get you nowhere. The smart thing to do instead when faced with a chaotic situation, is to take some time to identify the next steps and create a roadmap for yourself. By doing that, you can eliminate a lot of the uncertainty and fear that often come with uncertain situations.

This is why giving yourself breathing room, and pausing during chaotic situations, is an incredibly useful strategy.

Getting clear on what you need to do also means taking a step back and assessing the situation objectively. Sometimes you get so caught up in your emotions and the chaos of the moment that you lose sight of what's really important. But by taking a deep breath and assessing the situation from a more detached perspective, you can identify the key factors, issues and priorities.

I want you to picture this - you're on a cruise ship, and the captain tells you to grab the wheel. You look out at the vast expanse of water in front of you and feel a twinge of panic. All sorts of thoughts are running through your head, thoughts like what if you steer the boat in the wrong direction? Or, what if you hit a big rock and sink like the Titanic? Or, what if you steer the ship into a major storm?

But then the captain hands you a map, a compass, and a clear set of instructions. Suddenly, you feel calm, confident and in control. You know exactly what to do, where to go, and how to get there.

The same principle applies to your life as well. When you're feeling overwhelmed and your mind is in a state of chaos, it's easy to let your thoughts spiral out of control. But by getting clear on what you need to do, you can cut through the noise, get clarity and focus on what really matters.

That clarity can then help you break down even big, scary tasks into small, manageable steps. And when you do that, you can then prioritise what you need to do, and make sure that you're tackling the most important tasks first. This will also help you get rid of distractions and stay laser-focused on your next steps.

This brings me on to an important point - a very effective way to get clear on what you need to do is to break down the situation into smaller and more manageable steps. Doing this can make even a scary task seem a lot more manageable, and can give you more of a sense of progress and accomplishment along the way.

On that note, it's important to remember that progress doesn't always happen in big leaps. Most of the time, it's the small steps that add up to big changes.

As far as clarity is concerned, by getting clear on what you need to do, you're also giving yourself permission to say "no" to things that aren't aligned with your goals. You can say "no" to that social event that will drain your energy, or "no" to that work project that doesn't light you up. By setting clear boundaries, you're taking care of yourself and ensuring that you have the time and energy to focus you on what really matters.

Another key to getting clear on what you need to do is to communicate with others. Asking for advice from colleagues, friends, or family members can give you a fresh perspective and can also help you see the situation in a new light.

Here is a strategy regarding this that can really help - get someone to bounce ideas off of, or even to share the burden of decision-making. Doing this will take away a lot of the pressure, and make it easier for you to do what you need to do in a cool, calm and collected way.

As Jimi Hendrix famously said, in order to change the world, you have to get your head together first. This isn't just true for the big goals and situations, it's also true for the regular day to day things. Getting your head together and staying cool, calm and collected is key to living a good life, and dealing with chaos effectively is a very important part of achieving that calm state of mind.

The more chaos you're dealing with, the harder it is to stay cool, calm and collected. Chaos really is one of the biggest obstacles to your ability to stay composed. That said, there are lots of things you can do to go from chaos to clarity, as you have learned in this chapter (and the earlier chapters). And when you put to practise what you've learned, it'll become easier to handle unexpected and even troublesome situations.

More importantly, applying what you've learned so far will help you go from chaos to clarity. And when you do that, you will find it easier to stay cool, calm and collected, even in the face of utter chaos.

Getting clear on what you need to do can be a powerful tool for staying calm, cool, and collected no matter the situation. By taking the time to assess the situation, break it down into manageable steps, and getting advice (or even help) from others, you can tackle any form of chaos with clarity, confidence and purpose.

Get a handle on the chaos in your mind. Because that will help you get clarity on what you need to do next, and stay cool, calm and collected no matter what. And the next time you find yourself feeling overwhelmed, take a step back, breathe, and ask yourself this: what do I need to do next?

The answer might surprise you.

...

Your Five Step Strategy

Action may not always bring happiness, but there is no happiness without action - William James

***

Congratulations, you've finished the book! From the importance of focusing on the present and self-care to the value of getting help and preparing for the unexpected, you've gained a wealth of knowledge and insights and strategies about how to deal with life's inevitable challenges, obstacles, and chaos.

That said, reading about these concepts is just the beginning. To truly benefit from what you've learned, you need to take action and apply what you've learned in your daily life.

To help you with that, here are five steps you can take to start implementing these strategies:

1. Practice mindfulness: Take some time each day to practise mindfulness. Whether it is through meditation, deep breathing, journaling, or just focusing on the present moment, mindfulness can help you stay centred and calm in the face of stress, chaos and anxiety.
2. Take care of yourself: Self-care isn't just a buzzword, it is essential for maintaining your physical, emotional and mental wellbeing. It's not complicated either. All you really need to do is make sure that you're getting enough sleep, eating healthy, staying fit, and engaging in activities that bring you joy and relaxation.
3. Ask for help when you need it: As you have learned, asking for help isn't a sign of weakness. If anything, it's a sign of strength. Whether you need to talk to a friend, family member, or professional, or need active help with something challenging, don't be afraid to reach out for support anytime you're struggling.

4. Plan ahead: While you can't always predict what challenges you'll face in the future, you can take steps to prepare yourself for whatever comes your way. Think through potential scenarios and develop a plan of action that you can turn to in times of stress.
5. Get clear on your goals: When you know what you want to achieve, it gets easier to stay level-headed, focused and calm, even in the middle of chaos. So take some time to reflect on your goals, and prioritise the actions that will help you get there.

Making these strategies part of your daily routine will take time and effort, but the rewards are well worth it. By practising mindfulness, taking care of yourself, getting help when needed, planning ahead, and getting clear on your goals, you'll be better equipped to handle life's challenges with grace and resilience.

Remember, staying cool, calm, and collected is a skill that can be developed, and no matter what your life situation is, you absolutely can develop this skill. So keep practising, and don't be afraid to ask for help along the way.

I wish you all the best.

NOTES

This Is Not the End

The journey of a thousand miles begins with one step - Lao Tzu

***

In today's fast-paced world, it's easy to feel overwhelmed by the daily demands of life. From unexpected challenges and chaotic situations to moments of joy, you all face a varied range of experiences that can (and does) affect your ability to stay cool, calm, and collected.

The good news is that there are a variety of strategies you can use to help you navigate these situations with strength, grace and ease. And you just learned quite a few of these. To give you a reminder, let's quickly go through the main points.

One of the keys to staying calm is to be proactive instead of reactive. Rather than waiting for problems to crop up, you can take steps to prepare yourself ahead of time.

By focusing on what truly matters, you can avoid getting bogged down by stress, confusion and worry, and instead stay focused and have a positive outlook that will help you tackle anything that comes your way. As the saying goes, it's better to see the glass half full than it is to see it half empty.

Of course, there are times when unexpected challenges will crop up despite your best efforts to prepare. That's where having a present focus will help. By taking the time to nurture your mind, body, and soul, you can cultivate the inner strength and resilience you need to stay centred and grounded no matter what life throws your way.

And if you still find yourself struggling, asking for help from others can be just what you need to help you regain your footing, and find a way forward.

Ultimately, staying calm, cool, and collected is all about getting clear on what you need to do, and making conscious decisions that align with your goals and values. By taking the time to think things through and making a plan, you can avoid the expectation trap and stay ahead of the game, even in the face of even the most worrying of circumstances.

With these strategies in mind, you can approach life with a sense of confidence, calm and ease, knowing that you have the tools that you need to handle anything that comes your way.

By the way, if you're unsure about any of these concepts, just go back and read the relevant chapter(s) again. That will help you effectively implement what you have learned, and help you take on whatever life throws at you.

To sum it up, staying calm in the face of challenging situations is no small feat, but it is possible. Whether you are focusing on self-care, asking for help from others, or simply getting clear on what you need to do, there are a variety of strategies you can use to stay focused, centred and grounded in the middle of life's ups and downs. And by embracing the unexpected, staying proactive, and nurturing your mind, body, and soul, you can effectively cultivate the inner strength and resilience you need to face any situation cool, calm and collected.

You now have the knowledge, insights and strategies that can (and will) help you face any situation - no matter how confusing, worrying or challenging - in a cool, calm and collected way. All you need to do now is apply what you have learned. Because applying what you have learned in this book is what will ultimately get you to the endpoint - to the point where you will **be chill - and be cool, calm and collected no matter what**.

Your Fast Checklist

Here is a checklist to help you apply in your own life what you have just learned:

1. Be proactive, rather than reactive.
2. Stay focused on what matters.
3. Look at the bright side, even if it is hard to find the positive.
4. Manage your expectations.
5. Embrace the unexpected, and stop trying to control everything.
6. Hope for the best but prepare for the worst.
7. Get clear on what you need to do.
8. Think before you act.
9. Take care of yourself.
10. Focus on the present.
11. Ask for help anytime you need it.

This list will also give you a quick reminder of what you have learned so far.

Review this checklist regularly, and make it a point to keep these in mind as much as possible. Because that will help you deal with even the most challenging of situations in a cool, calm and collected way.

As for the book, this is where your journey begins. You have just learned a ton of valuable insights. And now it is time to apply what you have learned. Because that is where the rubber will meet the road, and how you can use these insights to make a positive difference in your life.

Get started.

Before You Go…

Before you go, I have a favor to ask (youll, three actually)…

1. If you found this guide informative, **please leave a review** on Amazon because that helps this guide reach more people. Thanks in advance for your help!
2. Share the link to this guide with anyone who you think should know this.
3. Let me know what you found useful, and how it helped you in your life.

Hearing from my readers about the positive impact my work has on them keeps me going. I really do love hearing from my readers so do reach out with your experiences, feedback and suggestions.

Here's my email: growthphilosophypodcast@gmail.com (I reply to every email personally).

On a side note, if you have any suggestions about the guide, including any typos or errors that might be there, let me know. Just email with the word "suggestion".

That's it for this guide. I genuinely appreciate you taking the time to read through the guide, and I am excited about the positive impact it will have in your life when applied.

Thanks again, and all the best.

msalek

Salek

About the Author

M Salek is a multi-bestselling author, award winning philanthropist, mindset coach and peak performance strategist. He's the host of the Better Mindset Show, a bite-sized weekly podcast show focused on empowering listeners to think better and upgrade their lives (the show was heralded as one of UK's top ten personal development podcasts in 2021/22).

Self improvement has been a lifelong passion (and mission) for Salek. He has spent decades studying the works of masters in all fields of self improvement and personal development, including spirituality, philosophy, and even the hard sciences like psychology and neuroscience.

That's literally thousands of books... over many, many years! All with the aim of personal growth and improvement, and helping others.

Now you can benefit from those years of knowledge and experience through his podcast, books and guides.

His mission is to help empower people to create a better life for themselves, and others. Join him on his mission. You can find more details on his website (mhasalek.com), facebook page, and even follow his twitter or instagram (@themsalek) for more tips, insights and hacks.

Find out more:
- Author's Website
- Other books by the author
- The Better Mindset Show - Learn how to improve your mind, and upgrade your life through this bite-sized weekly podcast.
- Facebook page - Get more tips and insights
- Private group and mastermind for smart thinkers
- Twitter and Instagram - For even more tips, hacks and insights

3 More Books

Here are 3 of my other books that you might also find useful:

- **Better Mindset: 15 Rules for a Better Mind, and Better Life -** There are very few things you can do in life and very few areas where minor adjustments can lead to major changes and major improvements more than making small changes in your mindset. Mindset is the critical leverage point that can completely transform one's life. This is why the best of the best always talk about mindset and how you think, and train their minds consistently, without fail. The people who reach the top work on their mind all the time because they know just how much it matters. And it matters, a LOT. Even the smallest improvements and adjustments in your mindset can help you experience big benefits and major improvements in your life, and that is what this book will help you to do. Get your copy here.
- **Radical Productivity: Master Your Time, Eliminate Procrastination, and Radically Improve Your Productivity -** Do you want to transform your productivity (and effectiveness)? Do you want to have more impact with your work? Are you ready to finally stop wasting your time and start making the most of it? If you said YES to any of these questions, then this book is for you. Get your copy here to get started.
- **The Business Launch Code: A Step By Step Guide To Starting Your Own Business -** In this beginner's business guide, you will get step by step instructions on what to do to get your business idea up and running, and it really is as simple as just following the steps, one at a time. You don't need to worry about figuring out what to do next or deal with any other such confusion. If you want to start your own business, then this is a must-read. Get your copy here.

You can find a full list of all my books (along with more details) here.

I wish you all the best with all your current and future goals.

Always remember...

Improve your mind to improve your life

www.ingramcontent.com/pod-product-compliance
Lightning Source LLC
Chambersburg PA
CBHW070457220526
45466CB00004B/1859